JAN
W9-DDC-752

DINOSAUR WORLD

Meat-eating Dinosaurs

Robin Birch

CHELSEA CLUBHOUSE

An Imprint of Chelsea House Publishers
A Haights Cross Communications Company

Philadelphia

This edition first published in 2003 in the United States of America by Chelsea Clubhouse, a division of Chelsea House Publishers and a subsidiary of Haights Cross Communications.

Chelsea Clubhouse
1974 Sproul Road, Suite 400
Broomall, PA 19008-0914

The Chelsea House world wide web address is www.chelseahouse.com

Library of Congress Cataloging-in-Publication Data

Birch, Robin.
   Meat-eating dinosaurs / by Robin Birch.
      p. cm. — (Dinosaur world)

Includes index.
Summary: Describes the appearance, eating habits, and habitat of meat-eating dinosaurs, including Tyrannosaurus, Deinonychus, Compsognathus, Gallimimus, and Baryonyx.

ISBN 0-7910-6987-7
1. Dinosaurs—Juvenile literature. 2. Predatory animals—Juvenile literature.
[1. Dinosaurs. 2. Predatory animals.] I. Title. II. Series.
QE861.5 .B57 2003
567.912—dc21

                                                                                    2002000842

First published in 2002 by
MACMILLAN EDUCATION AUSTRALIA PTY LTD
627 Chapel Street, South Yarra, Australia, 3141

Copyright © Robin Birch 2002
Copyright in photographs © individual photographers as credited

Edited by Angelique Campbell-Muir
Illustrations by Nina Sanadze
Page layout by Nina Sanadze

Printed in China

Acknowledgements

Department of Library Services, American Museum of Natural History (neg. no. 6744), p. 16; Auscape/ Francois Gohier, pp. 5, 12; The Field Museum (neg. no. GEO85818c), p. 7 (bottom); © The Natural History Museum, London, pp. 20, 25, 28; Royal Tyrrell Museum of Palaeontology/Alberta Community Development, p. 7 (top); Southern Images/Silkstone, p. 8.

While every care has been taken to trace and acknowledge copyright, the publisher tenders their apologies for any accidental infringement where copyright has proved untraceable.

Contents

Dinosaurs

Dinosaurs lived millions of years ago. There are no dinosaurs alive today.

We know dinosaurs lived because scientists have dug up and studied their bones.

Meat-eaters

Some dinosaurs ate animals and others ate plants. The dinosaurs that ate animals are called meat-eaters. Some meat-eating dinosaurs were huge and some were small.

Huge meat-eaters ate other dinosaurs. Small meat-eaters ate insects and other small animals. Most meat-eating dinosaurs had sharp teeth for catching and chewing their food. We can see their sharp teeth in their **skulls**.

Meat-eating dinosaurs had scales on their skin, as all other dinosaurs did. Snakes, lizards, and other **reptiles** that live today have scales on their skin, too.

Meat-eating dinosaurs lived both in forests and in places with few trees. They lived wherever there was food to be caught.

Tyrannosaurus

(tie-RAN-uh-SAWR-uhs)

Tyrannosaurus was one of the biggest meat-eating dinosaurs. It was as heavy as an elephant and stood about 20 feet (6 meters) tall.

Tyrannosaurus had three toes with strong claws on each foot. It had two fingers on each of its small arms. Each finger had a sharp claw.

Tyrannosaurus had a huge head with strong **jaws** up to 4 feet (1.2 meters) long. It had as many as 60 long, sharp teeth that it used for grabbing and cutting food. When a tooth fell out, another one grew in its place.

Tyrannosaurus used only its mouth and feet
to catch its **prey**. Its arms were too short to
grab animals. Tyrannosaurus could eat up to
500 pounds (230 kilograms) of food in one bite.

13

Deinonychus

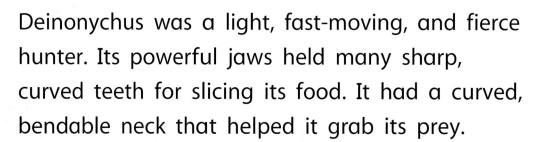

(die-NON-ih-kuhs)

Deinonychus was a light, fast-moving, and fierce hunter. Its powerful jaws held many sharp, curved teeth for slicing its food. It had a curved, bendable neck that helped it grab its prey.

Deinonychus had a long, **stiff** tail that helped it stay balanced and make fast turns. Its long arms each had three fingers that it used to hold onto its prey.

15

The skeleton of this dinosaur shows that one claw on each foot was long and curved. Deinonychus could bend this claw back and then swing it down quickly to stab an animal.

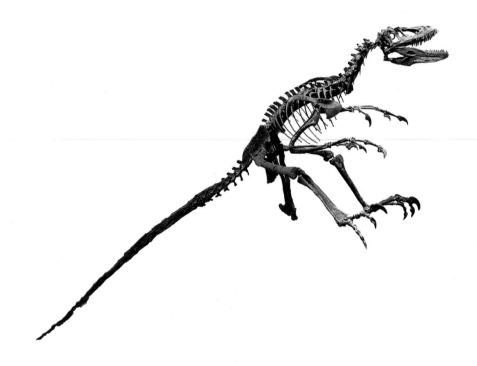

These dinosaurs probably hunted in groups called **packs**. They searched forests and open country for prey. They probably attacked a large dinosaur by jumping on it together to make the kill.

17

Compsognathus

(komp-sog-NAY-thus)

Compsognathus was a tiny dinosaur about the size of a chicken. It could run very fast on its two long, thin legs.

This dinosaur had two clawed fingers on each short arm. It had a long, straight tail that helped it stay balanced when it ran.

Compsognathus probably lived in dry areas with low-growing plants. Scientists have found its **skeleton** buried in rock. The skeleton is a **fossil**.

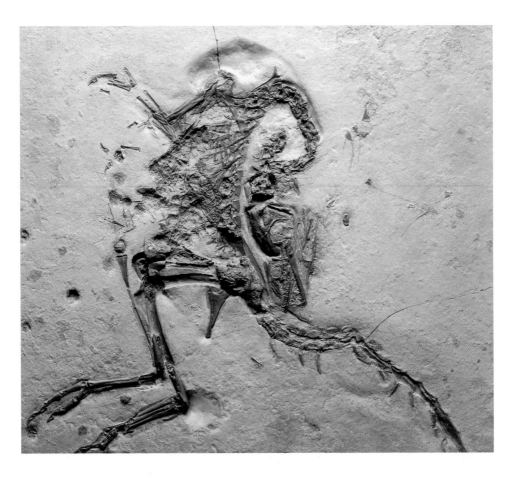

Compsognathus had a long, narrow head
and many sharp, spiky teeth. It probably
caught and ate insects, small lizards, and
small furry animals the size of mice.

Gallimimus

(gal-uh-MY-muhs)

Gallimimus was a tall, **slender** dinosaur. It had a long neck for a meat-eater and a long stiff tail. It could hold its head up high to watch for other dinosaurs that might attack.

Gallimimus had short arms with three fingers on each hand. It probably used its hands to help catch small animals.

Gallimimus had long, thin legs, which helped it run very fast. This dinosaur looked like today's ostrich and probably ran like one, too. It lived on dry land and walked along riverbanks to find food.

Gallimimus had a small head and a long, flat beak with no teeth. It probably ate small lizards, large insects, and dinosaur eggs. It swallowed its food whole.

25

Baryonyx

(bare-ee-ON-iks)

Baryonyx was a large dinosaur with a long neck and a long, stiff tail. It had a head like a crocodile.

Baryonyx had strong, **muscular** legs. Its front legs were only a little shorter than its back legs. Scientists are not sure whether Baryonyx walked on two or four legs.

Many small, pointed teeth filled Baryonyx's narrow jaws. Baryonyx probably lived near rivers where it could find fish to eat. Its long jaws and sharp teeth would have been good for grabbing slippery fish.

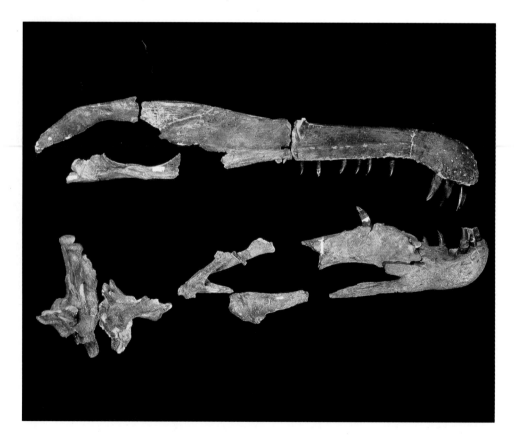

Baryonyx had huge curved claws on its hands that were 12 inches (30 centimeters) long. It may have used these claws for lifting fish out of the water. Baryonyx is the only known dinosaur that ate fish.

Names and Their Meanings

"Dinosaur" means "terrible lizard."

"Tyrannosaurus" means "**tyrant** lizard."

"Deinonychus" means "terrible claw."

"Compsognathus" means "pretty jaw."

"Gallimimus" means "chicken mimic."

"Baryonyx" means "heavy claw."

Glossary

fossil   something left behind by a plant or animal that has been preserved in the earth; examples are dinosaur bones and footprints.

jaw   the bones in the head that hold teeth

muscular   having large, well-developed muscles

pack   a group of animals that hunt together

prey   an animal that is hunted by other animals for food

reptile   a cold-blooded animal that breathes air through its lungs, lays eggs, and has scales

skeleton   the bones that support and protect an animal's body

skull   the bones of the head

slender   slim or thin

stiff   does not bend

tyrant   a cruel or unjust ruler

Index